I0697661

Corporations' Responsibility to Society

Patriotism over Profits

by

Al Craig Fleming

DORRANCE
PUBLISHING CO
EST. 1920
PITTSBURGH, PENNSYLVANIA 15238

The contents of this work, including, but not limited to, the accuracy of events, people, and places depicted; opinions expressed; permission to use previously published materials included; and any advice given or actions advocated are solely the responsibility of the author, who assumes all liability for said work and indemnifies the publisher against any claims stemming from publication of the work.

All Rights Reserved
Copyright © 2021 by Al Craig Fleming

No part of this book may be reproduced or transmitted, downloaded, distributed, reverse engineered, or stored in or introduced into any information storage and retrieval system, in any form or by any means, including photocopying and recording, whether electronic or mechanical, now known or hereinafter invented without permission in writing from the publisher.

Dorrance Publishing Co
585 Alpha Drive
Pittsburgh, PA 15238
Visit our website at *www.dorrancebookstore.com*

ISBN: 978-1-6366-1218-8
eISBN: 978-1-6366-1808-1

Corporations' Responsibility to Society

To make a reasonable profit for the shareholders

Utah Senator Mitt Romney so famously stated, "Corporations are people, my friend." That statement is mostly true since corporations are born with the filing for a corporate charter. Under ideal situations, the corporation grows and prospers.

Ultimately, many corporations die either voluntarily or involuntarily.

However, many corporations never die unlike humans. This one distinction is hugely significant since the corporation can accrue wealth, power and influence in perpetuity, making it virtually impossible to compare it to the limited lifespan of people. The social impact of large, multi-generational, multi-national corporations has a tremendous impact on the societies in which they operate for good or bad.

Most corporations have a positive impact on the communities and our nation as well. Until the recent income tax law changes, many paid reasonable Federal income taxes. A significant part of CEOs pay is based on the net profit as an incentive to enhance profitability which manifests through stock options. Higher profits and higher stock prices equals more money to the shareholders and the CEOs.

As recently as the 1980s, most Fortune 500 companies provided employee pensions, stock plans, and medical insurance. Now you get a 401(k) with a six-percent employer match of your contribution if you are lucky. Insurance is paid by the employee at a reduced rate. Average CEO pay in large multinational corporations is 600 times that of the average employee of the corporation. When luxury jet and sea planes owners grab economic stimulus funds needed to keep small businesses afloat, raw capitalism seems immoral.

Corporations should contribute to the public good

The CEO is rewarded primarily for

enhancing shareholder value while managing risk. Since fewer than forty percent of Americans own stock either directly or through a retirement account, the majority of the population is left out. Eighty-seven percent of the value of stocks are owned by high-income individuals. A third incentive should be added. Corporations should make a concerted effort to contribute to the public good. The corporation derives a tangible benefit from the consumer regardless of their employment status with the corporation.

To reward good behavior and to discourage bad behavior, companies could be rewarded with tax credits or tax deductions for bringing jobs back to the United States. Conversely, companies should have a higher tax burden when jobs are shipped out of the country. Any additional benefits or costs would fall to the bottom line, impacting the stock price accordingly.

Another way for corporations to contribute to the public good is to provide liberal benefits to employees. Benefits such as paid family leave, employee education programs, community service programs, and a living wage would have an immediate positive contribution to the public's benefit. Employee medical and psychological benefits should be provided by the Federal government for the purpose of gaining the maximum economies of scale that only the Federal government can provide. Corporations should have the option of providing such insurance benefits if it chooses. Corporations paying low wages should not be allowed to shift the social burden to society. A "Win-Win" transaction will be created between corporations and society to the benefit of all.

Corporations should help grow the GNP while taking into account the negative impact to society for their actions

The Federal government and corporations should work in partnership to the benefit of the greater good for the U.S.

While not advocating for Socialism, Capitalism with a conscience should be the norm. It is not so different from our current system except that it would put the average American citizen on a more equal footing with the large and medium-sized corporations. With our current system, profits are private but major losses are public. Overpaid corporate CEOs pay out their free cashflows to increase profits and reward themselves knowing that the Federal government will bail them out. Risk management is an afterthought at this point.

Public spending should be aimed at increasing the size of the American economic pie targeting those citizens who are more likely to spend money that is received. By adhering to this policy, consumption and the gross national product (GNP) would increase. Money has velocity, which means one dollar that changes hands four times has a "four-dollar" benefit to the economy. A dollar spent on a potential consumer without an immediate need will not be spent immediately.

Government spending for the benefit of corporations should be targeted toward those that create jobs or other societal benefits that can be quantified. Public/private partnerships should be created to train and hire from underserved communities. Corporations should implement job training programs to fill needed positions.

No! Greed is not good! Greed divides the "haves" and the "have nots." It divides us as Americans. Capitalism vs. Patriotism is the real argument when discussing large corporations and social responsibility. Profit maximization is often at odds with patriotism and profit maximization usually wins. What is needed is an objective look at the benefits of our current capitalistic system and examine areas where it could be improved to the benefit of more Americans. How can we use capitalism to expand the pie so more Americans can get a piece of it? CEOs are paid far too much for what they provide; the average worker is paid far too little for what they provide.

Any CEO whose company requires a bailout should be required to resign or significantly reduce their salary as a condition of the bailout. After all, effective risk management includes maintaining adequate capital and financial reserves to weather an unforeseen storm. Before a CEO can enhance shareholder value, he or she must ensure that the corporation can continue to operate as a going concern.

The stock market does not provide a level playing field for the average citizen

Equity transactions (stocks and stock options) in the stock market favor high income individuals. Dark pools, high-frequency trading, stock buybacks, and the IPO process all favor large, influential and sophisticated investors. This phenomenon occurs because large corporations have used their influence over the decades. For example, JPMorgan Chase has been in business since the Middle Passage, so their influence is multi-generational. The playing field should be leveled to allow more Americans to benefit from what should be the purest form of Capitalism.

The esoteric nature of many complicated financial instruments makes it impossible for many investors to participate in sections of the stock market that are particularly lucrative.

Moreover, the esoteric nature of certain investment vehicles is a breeding ground for fraud and manipulation. The prime example is the infamous "credit default swap," which was notorious for its role in the financial crisis of 2008.

Accountants and professionals in the mortgage brokerage/financial industries are aware of 'TBD' mortgage instruments, that trade inside of mutual and pension funds. 'TBD' is an acronym for "To Be Determined" and it is a component inside a mortgage instrument. The various tranches inside mortgage backed securities helped to conceal many risky mortgages prior to the financial crisis of 2008. TBAs and other comparable securities led to the bailout of the greedy corporations who caused and later benefited from the

American people who suffered the greatest losses resulting from the crisis.

Certain industries or certain components of particular industries should be overseen by a truly independent entity that is free of political bias or manipulation. It should have certain mandates that favor the interests of ordinary Americans. In the case of the stock market, the market-making role should be done by such an entity. The entity could be comparable to the Federal Reserve Board in the case of the stock market.

The market-making activity role would be done in a way that would allow average investors to benefit by allowing more than just large corporations and sophisticated investors to buy initial public offerings (IPOs) at the IPO price.

Under the current concept, average investors are forced to buy at a higher and more volatile price. The investment risk for market makers (large corporations) and sophisticated investors is low by comparison.

Activities associated with high frequency trading and dark pools should be curtailed to help even the playing field. Hedge funds and market manipulators are permitted to place servers close to the trading floors to their benefit. The treatment of carried interest for taxes should be abolished. The income and net worth requirements for options trading should be relaxed. The stock market does not produce a tangible product other than money and the rules have the effect of limiting the average investor. Dark pools are invisible to the average

American, but they are a legal means of generating large sums of money in secret. That can't be good.

The Swedish model

The country of Sweden provides its citizens social security, affordable healthcare, strict gun laws, five weeks paid annual leave, and a year of maternity leave. Prescription drugs have an annual cap of $210. A stay at the hospital for one night is $10. Sweden is not a communist or even a strictly socialist country. Sweden is a form of democratic socialism that should be emulated.

Ameliorating Society

We should implement a Marshall Plan for America that begins with rebuilding America's infrastructure as a means of providing needed economic stimulus to the economy. It will provide needed jobs for Americans while increasing tax revenues that will accompany the increased economic activity. What is being advocated is supply-side economics from the bottom up. The economy will be further stimulated because more money will flow to the people who would put it right back into the domestic economy. It will have the residual effect of raising the overall standard of living through the value of work.

The objective is to improve the overall American standard of living. To meet the objective, we must expand the domestic labor pool for the jobs that would be created through the infrastructure project. Nationwide training programs to provide the needed domestic workforce must be at the center of the project to ensure that training and work is available for those who are willing and able to accept the challenge. Corporations can establish or fund nonprofits to provide qualified dependable employees for hard-to-fill positions.

America can't be "THAT SHINING CITY ON A HILL" if She is not an autonomous nation. To build America, we must buy American even when it may not be "as" profitable. Globalization is good but America's economy had its genesis on the concept of Mercantilism.

The concept is that if you export more than you import you will achieve a favorable balance of trade, increasing the America standard of living.

Corporate decisions are based on maximizing profits without regard to anything else. From a purely economic perspective, every dollar that leaves the United States decreases the United States standard of living by one dollar.

There are 2.3 trillion dollars of low-hanging fruit in the form of the recent tax cuts that benefited large public corporations and the truly rich. The corporate tax rate should be increased to at least 38% and the corporate tax rate should be partiality based on revenue as well as profits. This feature would help ensure that large corporations pay their fair share of taxes. The estate tax should be reinstated to ensure those who have achieved the most will leave something to the nation that made it all possible.

The greatest transfer of wealth in the history of the world started with financial crisis of 2008 and it continues to this day. Wall Street caused the crisis because of their ravenous greed. During the depth of the Covid-19 crisis, large public and nonpublic corporations stepped in front of small and medium-sized companies knowing that America was on Her knees and needed those companies to survive. People are patriotic, but patriotism is not in the articles of incorporation or the mission statement of corporations.

Democracy relies on a well-educated population to flourish, so it is imperative that our education system be reformed beginning with higher teacher pay and a longer school year. Vocational education should be an option as well as advanced credits for college while in high school. Vocational schools at all levels would collaborate with businesses to ensure that students are being provided needed skills for employers seeking qualified personnel.

Economics, nutrition and government should be taught in high school to help develop life skills that will make for a more informed and productive workforce and citizen. Food processing has become so consolidated that only one of the five multi-national food processors in the U.S. is domestically owned. Moreover, our school lunch programs are geared toward maximizing profits by emphasizing carbohydrates instead of a healthier diet for children during their formative years when lifelong habits are instilled. The parents pass on bad eating habits to their children.

It is the main cause of obesity because those children become adults with bad eating habits that lead to a strain on the nation's health system, resulting in higher costs for all of us. Heart disease, diabetes, high blood pressure, kidney disease and obesity are mostly diet related.

If the profit motive were removed from school lunch programs, the benefits would be enormous. Large corporations lobby school districts to get the most profitable products in the schools. As a result, children cannot choose what is healthy to eat. Clearly, the best way to ensure that our children eat a healthy diet is to limit their options when those who have the power to make the determination are not around.

The Culture War

Liberty means freedom from oppressive authority. As a civil society, certain laws are expected. "Your freedom ends where my nose begins," would make most of our disagreements moot. We can't be exceptional if we can't engage in civil conversation. Whether you are Liberal, Moderate or Conservative, we all value our individual freedoms. Government is too big until we need good and big government. We will never attract the best people to government if government is vilified. At the national level, we should begin with term limits and getting money out of the process. Congress should be a place you go to serve for a specific term, not a place to get rich and retire in Congress.

Liberty means citizens can indulge in behaviors of which you may not agree but it is their right as long as it does not infringe on your ability to enjoy life, liberty and the pursuit of happiness. If hate is in your heart, it should not compel you to act on it because it is anti-American. Our quality of life requires that we respect one another's liberties. If we recognize that there are producers and consumers in our population and our economy, we can achieve a level of synergy that will accrue to the greater society.

When all is said and done, life is about choices and people usually get what they put into life. Let farmers grow as much as possible and find a way to feed the world profitably. We should endeavor to improve workers' rights as a means of increasing the size of the middle class in America. Income inequality is real and there would be less division amongst us if we all feel like we are a part of the American dream. We should be too busy to hate, and too busy to worry about whether your achievement somehow undermines my ability to do the same.

The United States of America is the only industrialized nation that ties medical care to employment. If you lose your job, you have no medical care. Overall mental and physical health would improve if healthcare wasn't motivated by the profit motive. The full purchasing power of the nation should be used to drive down healthcare and drug costs. That would help provide the means to provide healthcare to all Americans.

To provide the skilled professionals for healthcare and other industries in need of qualified professionals, colleges and universities should find a way to make college more affordable. The student loan burden should not act as a deterrent to attracting the best and the brightest to the medical profession. Hospitals should not be large corporations with the profit motive overriding quality/necessary medical care. Preventive care is far less costly than a visit to the emergency room.

The class, socioeconomic divide, religious and racial divide will have to be addressed in some form. One can accept that there is a part of human nature to gravitate toward people that we can relate to socially and at a cultural level. Liberty requires that we accept the concept of liberty for all regardless of our own personal prejudices. Feelings and personal prejudices cannot be legislated or controlled, but how we respond to others is legislated and controlled by societal norms. Those who adhere to those norms have all the right to liberty and the pursuit of happiness as anyone else.

The racial divide is real, and we must address it to recognize our true potential as a nation. Thomas Jefferson said, "There would never be racial harmony is the U.S. because the White man had committed so many atrocities against the Black man that forgiveness was impossible." During my football playing days, our team was one of a few integrated teams in Texas during the late 60s and early 70s. We won at least 90% of the games that we played against all-White or all-Black teams. The best teams that we played were integrated. We won because of our diversity. America "as a melting pot" is a noble precept but that very precept is viewed as a troubling concern for many. The fact of the matter is that Black Americans just want equal treatment under the law, and the opportunity to recognize their potential. Forgiveness is in the hearts of Black Americans if hate is not present by certain Whites who seek to persecute them individually and as a community.

Black Americans provided the labor needed to build the great American economy and the initial infrastructure that allowed us to be a true economic superpower. Cotton was the export commodity that allowed for the concept of mercantilism. Other cash crops such as tobacco, sugar, rice and other agricultural products were at the heart of the colonial economy. Black Americans left rural America to help fuel the industrial revolution and many achieved middle-class status and beyond. Once Black Americans won the right to vote, there was a Black renaissance of prosperity in America followed by White backlash.

Whatever White America doesn't like about Black Americans is attributable to obstacles placed before the Black family from slavery to Jim Crow laws and mass incarceration. Systemic racism is at the heart of what is wrong with the Black America. Racism, poverty, desperation and crime are close cousins. Systemic racism has been imbedded throughout American society since its inception. Black Americans sought the right to vote in 1866, again in 1957 and 1964 before the Voting Rights Act was passed and signed by President Lyndon B. Johnson. Unfortunately, the voting rights of Black Americans have been eliminated by the current Republican party, and voter suppression was again the order of the 2020 election cycle.

Since racism is mostly an economic construct, its logical result is poverty for the victims. Poverty leads to desperation. Desperate people are more likely to commit crime regardless of race, religion or national origin. The best deterrent to crime in the long run is opportunity. Four hundred years of oppression have taken its toll. Targeted investment in Black America would yield social and economic benefits to America while effectively closing the gap between the haves and have-nots. Investment could take the form of skills-training programs, education and revising the criminal justice system to mitigate racial bias. Dollars saved on incarceration should be redirected to community programs geared toward strengthening the Black family. Tax policy should be used to lessen the financial burden on Black Americans below certain economic thresholds.

America will never be great unless it provides for equal treatment to all of its citizens. Racism is both an economic and a social construct. It is literally the opposite of White privilege. Many Whites believe that when certain people prosper, they are somehow diminished. They may believe that the American pie is only so big. The more people fully participating in the economy, the economic pie gets bigger for all involved. Liberty means that we all have certain inalienable rights, so flag lovers need to really love and accept what the American flag stands for.

Corporations can play a critical role by investing in the Black community and providing economic opportunities in the form of philanthropy through job training and family stabilization programs. Entities that benefit from Black talent such as the NCAA should be required to give back to the Black community. Professional leagues such as the NFL, NBA, WNBA and MLB should expand their outreach programs. Tax policy should be used to encourage participation. Compassionate corporate greed is good. Diversity programs should be specifically targeted toward Black employees and Black-owned businesses. If corporations paid employees a living wage, both Blacks and all employees would benefit.

Racism and sexism are at the heart of our division. Those who will vilify a person based on their outward appearance are either ignorant, stupid or dumb. Such vilification is likened to a form of mental illness since it affects mood, thinking and behavior. Illogical thinking and behaviors are the hallmark of racism. Racists often claim Christianity or patriotism as a shield. They are by definition "not Christians" nor patriotic. At best they are blind hypocrites since they are not following the teachings of Jesus Christ and they are not living by the laws of the U.S. Constitution. True patriots believe in "Life, Liberty and the Pursuit of Happiness." Racists and everyone else are entitled to think what you think, but when anyone's liberty is violated, patriotism cannot be claimed as a rationale.

When police kill innocent Black Americans on a regular basis and face no consequences, it sends the message that there are two Americas and two systems of justice based solely on race. It sends a clear message that some Americans are not allowed to achieve the American dream if they don't look or speak a certain way. America has become a police state for some while allowing others to plunder and kill. Many police departments seem to have been infiltrated by an evil element that has more to do with "hunt down and kill" instead of 'protect and serve'. There are many good people who are in law enforcement; consequently, the culture in some departments is at the heart of the problem.

Police departments in many large cities act as an arm of hate groups bent of extracting harm to the Black communities they serve. The result is a sense of hopelessness and despair as promising lives are lost to those who should be there to protect those promising lives. Over time, the relationship between law enforcement and the Black community becomes adversarial in perception and in some cases, in fact. Those who are adversely impacted by police violence are even more disillusioned in their pursuit of the so-called American dream. Disillusionment devolves into depression, desperation and self-destructive actions that exacerbate their plight. All people should be able to live and not merely survive.

Women make up over fifty percent of the U.S. population and they should have the same economic opportunities as well as control of their bodies. There was a statistic that indicated that crime dropped significantly twenty years after the implementation of Roe vs. Wade. My logical mind tells me that women who choose to have children raise them better and it makes for a better society. Those who use "the sanctity of life" argument is a specious argument since those same individuals who are pro-life are often pro-death penalty.

The ideology that is pro-life is also opposed to providing healthcare and other services that would improve the quality of life for the born baby and the mother. Innocent lives are lost to gun violence daily and the obvious contradiction is never an issue. The same mostly male politicians who are "pro-life" will pay for an abortion for their mistress. Justice is not blind in the U.S. and the death penalty has sentenced too many innocent Americans to death even when the person's innocence was in doubt or obvious. The consequences of an unplanned pregnancy are totally different for a man compared to a woman. Having control over one's body is the ultimate liberty. Women's rights and civil rights are not mutually exclusive.

A loving two-parent household is the ideal, but we should allow for changes in male and female roles in the nuclear family. Insecure males need not fear the expanding accomplishments of woman in our society. Diversity of gender, race, class, religion and perspective makes for a more creative and productive society. Men and women should be expected to be active participants in child rearing.

Whatever relationships evolve should be respected if the goal of a stable nuclear family can be achieved.

While in the Las Vegas airport a few years back, a Latino airline employee who had been called to the baggage check-in told her English speaking co-worker that he should learn Spanish. The English speaking co-worker appeared puzzled by the comment. His pain could be felt. He had learned the King's English and now he was at a disadvantage in America (his native country) because he only spoke English. Speaking English wasn't enough for that situation. During a time of job searching, there was an advertisement for a job fair that had the heading "Diversity Job Fair, Bilingual only." All U.S. citizens should have the same opportunity in America if English is the primary language. The term American and 'U.S.' are used interchangeably.

We should secure our borders to maintain our national security, but immigrants should be treated with humanity and dignity. We need to know who is entering the country for security reasons while preserving the humanity of immigrants. Significant costs associated with medical and education result when large numbers of immigrants enter the country. Wages are driven down because companies and individuals take advantage of the immigrants' status; moreover, the laws of supply and demand naturally drive down wages. Greedy employers exploit the immigrant for the sake of a greater profit margin. Technology exists (E-Verify) to ensure that every employee is eligible to work in the U.S.

The solution is not to vilify those seeking the American dream, but to address the issues that are causing the immigrants to flee their homeland. Issues of the drug cartels and abject poverty are at the heart of the problem.

The best place to start is with the economic and justice systems. Life, liberty and the equal pursuit of happiness is codified in the Constitution. It is codified in Declaration of Independence that "all men are created equal."

Social media, for-profit news, and religious beliefs tend to exacerbate our differences. Like-minded people will always seek each other and that is expected. Social media companies and for-profit news organizations are large corporations making huge profits selling division and manipulating our behaviors toward large groups of Americans. Many Americans get their only news from these organizations and they are often subjected to false information and propaganda with the express intent of driving eyeballs and maximizing profit. The result is that people are hostile to others who are different or have a different opinion or belief.

Religious animosity has caused death and destruction since the beginning of time. Freedom of religion means that we tolerate all religions if those religions adhere to our social norms. Religious people who are intolerant of those who are agnostic are just as guilty of those who exhibit religious intolerance toward other religions. In the same vein that we have freedom of religion, we also have freedom from religion. Our liberty is put in jeopardy when religion beliefs of government are imposed on the people at large. Democracy relies on a well-informed and well-educated voter pool to make informed decisions based on logic and the greater good. The money changers are still in the temple.

There was a time in America when the news was not a profit-making part of media. News should be about presenting the facts of a story without personal bias. News should be about journalism and the presenter should avoid letting personal bias enter the story. Sensational journalism has the impact of driving Americans into their respective corners with the express purpose of increasing the ratings to drive advertising dollars. Since many Americans consume their news via social media, social media should be held to the same standard as mainstream media when it pertains to vetting the facts of a story.

The Earth Is Talking to Us!
Within the last 12 months, the world has experienced major fires, earthquakes, tornados, hurricanes, floods, droughts and a worldwide pandemic. Mother Earth is letting us know that we need to pay attention, and action must be taken now. Our nation's scientific achievements are directly linked to our overall standard of living. Most of the great companies in America are in the technology sector of the economy. If we are to remain great, we must insist on great government as well.

Government should be medium in size, but it should be nimble enough to be big when needed and small otherwise. Science tells us that the climate of the earth is warming but our leaders ignore the science partly because of politicians controlled by the fossil fuel industry. What is worse is the fact that the fossil fuel industry has the capital to help convert to clean energy, and they would achieve the same level of profits. Global warming has become another wedge issue along with abortion, the Second Amendment, and immigration policy.

We must address violence in America whether it's school shootings or gang violence. The obvious common denominator in the problem is guns. A well-armed militia may have been effective in colonial times, but if a well-armed militia were to confront the armed forces today it would lose. Guns are fine for protection or sport, but the legality of weapons of war in the streets of America must be addressed. Our children shouldn't have to fear for their lives at school and citizens shouldn't have to be concerned about armed gangs in impoverished communities. There is no 'so-called' slippery slope because assault-styled rifles were once banned and the slippery slope was not applicable.

The grief brought on by violence has the effect of multiplying the initial act leading to multiple broken lives and lifelong depression for many. Again, education is key. Effective communication and problem resolution should be taught in schools to help develop life skills to deal with complex situations to help mitigate conflicts. Conflict resolution training promotes rational thinking while taking into account the opinions of those who may have views that conflict with our own. We all have the right to be heard. We all have the right to be treated with respect and dignity; therefore, we should be willing to do and expect the same. "We should treat others the way we want to be treated."

Understanding those with conflicting opinions and views is key to bridging the divide in America. We should have the humility and self-awareness to enable those who have conflicting opinions to express those conflicts and views openly without judgement and consternation.

We should want each other to

succeed because the more successes, the more our nation prospers. Our quality of life improves as a result. Accept each other's differences and expect the same.

Covid-19

The Covid-19 pandemic has the effect of revealing the ugly under-belly of America. The wealth, economic and healthcare disparities lay bare as those who we rely on the most are paid the least. If we value work, we should pay those who work in essential jobs better. Essential workers are the ones we need for our basic needs. Capitalism needs a major adjustment. Not only should we move our supply chain back to the U.S. to provide jobs; we must ensure that we provide well-paying jobs to boost our economy.

The best way to help small businesses and the U.S. economy is to ensure that small businesses survive and prosper. Small businesses provide 80% of U.S. jobs and communities are diminished when large corporations take profits earned in a community or country and reinvest those profits elsewhere. Large corporations who reinvest in the communities and countries that they serve are the best examples that should be emulated. The best approach is to create synergy between businesses of all sizes to adapt an approach of responsibility as it relates to our society. Prosperity begets prosperity and the benefits would accrue to the greater society.

The concepts of universal healthcare would have lessened the death toll and anxiety associated with the pandemic, and universal income would have ensured economic stability. Those who need income to survive will spend immediately resulting in monetary velocity and a prosperous economy. Money provided to those who have what they need decreases the monetary velocity and is a drag on economic activity. Moreover, robotics, artificial intelligence (A-I), and other emerging technologies will require that we find new ways to empower those who are displaced as a result. The U.S. has a consumer-based economy so the definition of a job for displaced workers should be redefined to allow a modified version of universal basic income to be implemented. Displaced workers would provide needed services to the community and get compensated. The economy and the community benefits, and the dignity of work is preserved.

Soft-skill development should be required in schools to provide the skills required for tasks that technology cannot perform (soft human skills). Our diversity is our strength. When we value the humanities, we will value and compensate those who interface with people as much as we value CEOs or Wall Street moguls. Effective communication should be taught in middle schools to improve social skills and mitigate conflict. The high schools should teach sociology and economics to ensure a more rounded citizen.

We do not need big government; we need smart government. Liberty means that we live the life of our choice, so we should help to facilitate more choices. States should be granted more autonomy on issues such as abortion and gun rights. On the critical issues of our time, we will have to come to a resolution if we want to enjoy the dream. Politics should reflect the local community as much as possible to reflect the will of the people in those communities. Jerrymandering should be eliminated because it is allowing the politicians to choose their voters, which makes government accountable to dark money instead of the voters.

Twenty days in 2020

The murder of George Floyd in May of 2020 revealed the overt racism and police brutality in the U.S. for the world to see. We all saw a public lynching preceded by eight minutes of torture. It not only revealed racism in the U.S., but it revealed the U.S. as a police state and the inhumanity harbored by some police persons. Police routinely act as judge, jury and executioner with impunity. We were at a true crossroads because the public lynching was preceded by many others and it happened in the midst of a global pandemic.

Americans of all races came together to confront the injustices perpetrated on Black Americans daily and our better angels revealed themselves in a way that had not been seen before. Americans began to recognize that "Black Lives Matter" is not just a slogan, but a reality. Liberty means that no person is above the law. That means the President and that means the police. Police unions are more powerful than local elected officials and that is a major problem. We need to get to the point where police are there to protect and serve. The entire criminal justice system is fraught with systemic racism. Looting is unacceptable and so is police brutality; however, looting is often triggered by police brutality.

National standards for police conduct should be updated to make the police accountable to the community. The police department budget should include mental health responders. Traffic stops should be minimized by changing the process using computers and recording the license plates of offenders and providing ticketing and court dates by mail. The police would be able to provide more security with fewer officers. Savings in the police budget would provide more funds to allocate to social services or community programs designed to improve the quality of life of the citizens. Community policing should be the order of the day.

Coming together as a nation

The best place to start is with economic equality and criminal justice reform. Life, liberty and the equal pursuit of happiness is codified in the Constitution.

If Amazon, Google, Apple, Facebook and Findface collaborate, we have no privacy. Computer issues exacerbate the problem by erroneously identifying the wrong person. Facial recognition software is more accurate when the face of Whites is scanned, but more incorrect identifications occur when the faces of Blacks are scanned. In addition, law enforcement and the government can use the service in a way that ends with unintended consequences. Liberty is jeopardized when privacy is lost. Many Black Americans have already lost their liberty and everyone else could be next. A corrupt or incompetent government with unpatriotic intent can destroy our Democracy and our freedoms. Demonstrators can be harassed or rounded up. The worst part of the collaboration is that it could result in surreptitious mind control that would ensure election results among other negative outcomes. Again, there is no liberty if there is no privacy.

Clearview International allows, in real-time, Law enforcement to gain access to the entire body of a citizen's life that is known by Governments as well as many companies with malice as a business plan. The Clearview business plan makes Mark Zuckerberg and Facebook seem like a regular corporation with a noble intent.

Capitalism is a good thing; but greedy, unscrupulous capitalist give capitalism a bad name. Capitalism combined with compassion would be a great thing (i.e. compassionate capitalism), and it is not socialism. There is already a mechanism in place to address corporate responsibility to society. It is called Environmental, Social and Governmental (ESG). The environment will provide a cleaner planet while creating jobs for the 21st century and expanding the economy. The social component will provide inclusion and many other societal benefits including synergies that can't be quantified. The government has the role of facilitating the environment and the social parts.

There are many corporations that exhibit the characteristics needed going forward. In fact, I had the privilege of working for such a corporation when I graduated college. The founder was an urbane visionary with altruistic traits. The company was also the industry leader with a diverse and talented workforce. It attracted the best and the brightest because of the corporate culture and the outstanding benefits. The company was extremely profitable and achieved outstanding acclaim because of its innovations. It was a paragon of compassionate capitalism.

Our politics are the main expression of our divisions. When we choose our leaders, we should be mindful of their ideology, intellect, integrity, empathy and positive leadership skills. Our nation's leaders should model behaviors that we hold dear; however, we must get the money out of politics as much as possible. The election cycles should be shortened to allow more time for governing and less time on fundraising. Government should be for the people, not for the people with money and influence. The Democratic and the Republican parties are so far apart ideologically that no real legislation gets done that would actually move the nation forward in a meaningful way.

The United States leads the world in science and technology, yet many of our national leaders don't believe in science. Economic prosperity and climate change initiatives need not be mutually exclusive objectives. We need leaders who are willing to govern with the peoples' interest instead of the interest of their corporate donors. The increase in the national minimum wage should be tied to the increase in congressional pay. Presidential candidates should be required to release their tax returns and to submit to an IQ test. The President of the United States should be competent, patriotic, compassionate and free of the potential of financial manipulation. America should lead by example, not by bullying. Our standing and respect around the world is measured by our humanity and it is punctuated by our might.

Our moral authority to lead is largely based on how we treat the least among us. If we can merge the stated values of the former Republican Party (family values, fiscal responsibility and a nation of laws) into the virtues of the

Democratic Party, American would live up to its creed. The stated virtues of the Democratic Party are inclusion, investment in science and technology, and the recognition that corporations have a responsibility to society.

Covid-19 and Corporate Greed

The Covid-19 pandemic dealt a devastating blow to families and the economy writ-large both in the U.S. and worldwide. The pandemic revealed the major disparities that have always existed with the U.S. economic model. Employees that were deemed essential were those who are paid the lowest pay and assumed the greatest risk during the pandemic. Essential to our very survival are those jobs involving food, sanitation, transportation, education and public safety. Major disparities in health were also exposed and should be addressed by ensuring affordable healthcare that is not tied to employment.

Higher-paid jobs and professions were more likely to be able to work from home. The debate concerning the need for a living wage is always countered with the argument that companies would hire fewer employees if the minimum wage were raised. The argument doesn't hold up with the economic law of supply and demand. If employees were paid higher wages, those employees could consume more and increase the demand for a whole host of goods and services throughout the economy. The only potential negative impact of higher wages for large corporations is reduced profit margins, which can be overcome with increased sales.

The following paragraphs are real-life cases/examples of the aforementioned precepts in real-time:

Walmart, Incorporated reported earnings per share (EPS) of $1.27 in the second quarter of 2019. In the second quarter of 2020, Walmart, Incorporated reported EPS of $1.56 on an accelerated basis. EPS accelerated even though Walmart increased employee pay during the pandemic and incurred increased costs as a result of implementing social distancing during the quarter.

Target Companies, Incorporated reported ESP of $1.82 in the second quarter of 2019. In the second quarter of 2020, Target Companies, Incorporated reported EPS of $3.35.

Like Walmart, Target Companies, Incorporated incurred increased costs as a result of increased employee pay and social distancing. Target implemented curbside pickup and other measures that added costs.

The corporations' earnings were bolstered by government stimulus that provided the means for consumers to have the necessary spending that benefited the bottom line of the corporations. The increased pay will result in increased tax revenue to the Federal Government. Corporate spending in the form of labor costs increases consumer spending, which in turn increases corporate earnings, which provide benefits to society in the form of economic growth. The pie gets bigger for all involved.

Walmart, Incorporated is a prime example of corporate greed. It does not pay associates (employees) a living wage, so many of Walmart's employees rely on government assistance to make ends meet. The employees then buy groceries from Walmart, Incorporated using government assistance, thus benefiting the corporation. The net effect is that We (the American people) are subsidizing one of the wealthiest families in the world.

Income inequality is an ancillary threat to our democracy, and the income gap gets wider with each financial crisis. The greatest redistribution of wealth occurred during the financial crisis of 2008 and it is occurring now during the Covid-19 pandemic. The wealth redistribution occurs from the have-nots to the haves. The most egregious example of corporate greed happened when the "Payroll Protection Program" (PPP) was implemented to provide money for small businesses to retain employees, pay rent, and remain viable during the pandemic. During the initial phase of the program, the money was exhausted because large corporations, wealthy companies and individuals received large government-sponsored loans and grants while smaller, less viable companies were left out of the program. Grant money was provided to the large airlines and other large corporations that are notorious for extreme executive pay and major stock buybacks over the past decade. The airlines have bought back stock in the amount of $45.5 billion since the financial crisis of 2008. The airlines have been bailed three times during my lifetime. This is the definition of ongoing corporate welfare.

Although money was provided by the government, the companies did not accept it because of limitations including stock buybacks and executive pay. The Federal Reserve is also buying corporate debt as a means of propping up large companies during the pandemic. No such support is given to small businesses, which account for over eighty percent of jobs in the U.S. As a result, it is estimated that up to forty percent of small businesses will be lost for good. Corporate socialism is alive and well in the U.S. because corporate profits are private and corporate losses are public in a crisis.

Government is controlled by corporate interest so nothing will change until money is not considered free speech. Politicians are beholding to large corporate donors instead of we the people. Congress provided a $1.3 trillion tax cut to large corporations during a robust economy, but Congress is unwilling to provide economic stimulus payments to individuals who lost jobs during the pandemic. Many corporations with revenues in the billions of dollars pay no taxes while the average American's taxes stayed the same or increased. When left to their own devices, large corporations will do whatever they can to maximize profits, including government payoffs through lobbyists. Corporate welfare is a real thing and it benefits almost all industries, including energy (oil), pharmaceutical, and insurance.

Environmental, Society and Governmental (ESG)

Corporate responsibility to society was a prevalent theme during the 1970s and 1980s. As corporations gained more power and influence, the theme was replaced with the concept of maximizing shareholder value, which exists to this day. Recently, more enlightened executives of large corporations have begun to address the imbalances in our society by expanding the corporate mission statement to include environmental, societal, and governance (ESG) issues as well.

Our economy will be energized by addressing the challenges of climate change since it will allow for the creation of new well-paying jobs for the under and unemployed. The governmental role is that of a facilitator by enacting programs for job training, tax policies, healthcare, and infrastructure. ESG gives conscientious executives cover to do the right thing even when shareholder value is impacted adversely. Corporations should bring our manufacturing jobs back to the U.S. and pay a living wage when they do. Our country is their most valuable stakeholder. Corporations are at the center since they are uniquely qualified and capable of facilitating the change needed to implement ESG. The net beneficiary of ESG programs is our society and the world. We will be in a better place for all to realize their potential and to have liberty as stated in the Constitution.

Synergy and our moral authority to lead

Synergy is the interaction of two or more organizations, substances, or other agents to produce a combined effect greater than the sum of their separate effects. Expressed in purely mathematical terms, $1+1=3$ or more. We solve the problems of the environment by confronting the problem as an opportunity to retool the economy with new high-paying green jobs. Improving our aging infrastructure including broadband and 5G technology will further enhancing job and economic growth. If we can get past our racial and socioeconomic divide, American can realize its true productive and creative potential unleashing a fourth industrial revolution that would propel our gross nation product (GNP) into the stratosphere.

When we take back our government so it again reflects the will of the people instead of the rich and powerful, we can once again be that "SHINING CITY ON A HILL." Only then can we regain our moral authority to lead the world into a new era of peace and prosperity.

www.ingramcontent.com/pod-product-compliance
Lightning Source LLC
Chambersburg PA
CBHW070042260726
48658CB00002B/687